C000132041

TELL ME WHO WE WERE
BEFORE LIFE MADE US

An Anthology

Published in 2021 by
3 of Cups Press
London

Copyright Individual Poems © 2021

Marisca Pichette, Donika Kelly, R. Bratten Weiss, Alexander Walker,
Peehu, S. Rupsha Mitra, Ojo Taiye, Lucy Peters, Jenny Mitchell, Abduljalal
Musa Aliyu, Bal, afshan d'souza-lodhi, Nicola Geddes, Charlie Kite, Molly
Beale, Anne Chafer, Jenny Blackford, Lea Harper, Arun Jeetoo, Jay Délise,
Manahil Bandukwala, Anna Kate Blair, Jonathan Kinsman, Kait Quinn,
C.B. Blanchard, Maroula Blades, Oakley Flanagan, Jane Flett,
mandla rae, Sophia Freire

The right of to be identified as the creators of this work has been asserted
by the creators in accordance with the Copyright, Designs and
Patents Act 1988.

All rights reserved. Except for brief quotations in a review, this book, or
any part thereof, may not be reproduced, stored in or introduced into a
retrieval system, or transmitted, in any form or by any means, electronic,
mechanical, photocopying, recording or otherwise, without the prior
written permission of the publisher.

References to websites were correct at the time of writing.

Paperback ISBN 9781916263925
eBook ISBN 9781916263949

Printed and bound by CPI Group (UK) Ltd, Croydon, CR0 4YY

Edited by Maz Hedgehog
Cover design by Ambereen Khan
Cover art by Xhi Ndubisi
Typeset by Laura Jones

www.3ofcups.co.uk

CONTENTS

CONTENT NOTES

INTRODUCTION

Maz Hedgehog

When I first submitted to 3 of Cups' anthology, *On Relationships*, I never imagined that I would still be working with them more than two years later. More has changed than I could have possibly predicted, and this anthology is no different. This is not a book about the pandemic. That said, this isn't a book I expected to be editing from my bedroom.

In a year where I – like so many – have felt unmoored and unprepared and entirely out of my depth, it was fitting I would take on a project that pushed me so far beyond my comfort zone.

In reading the submissions, I had the painful task of saying no to so many poems: poems I liked, poems that moved me, poems that made me laugh. It wasn't until I figured out that my "no" was more a "not now" and "not here", that I was able to let myself fall in love with the process. In turn, I fell in love with the project. Each poem in here is one that changed me a little, one I couldn't stop thinking about, or one that I had to go back and read again and again.

Tell Me Who We Were Before Life Made Us is a book about history, sort of. It is a book about the stories that made us who we are, the ones we know shape us and the ones we don't. Poems like *Overture Con Sordina* by Jon Kinsman address the uglier parts of family history, whilst *Exordium: Dramatis Personae* by Molly Beale look at the uglier parts of British history. But, it is not all grim; *Herb of the Sun* by Jay Délise and *Dragon* by Alexander Walker are brimming with joy and good humour and feel something like home.

I hope in reading this anthology you will be moved as I was, and connect with parts of yourself you may have neglected for a while. I hope that, as you face a new day/year/decade, these poems will make you think a little differently about our histories, how they are shaped and changed by each new telling. I hope that you, like me, will find these poems a source of strength and inspiration on harder days and in darker nights.

Tell Me Who We Were Before Life Made Us is a collaborative effort, just as life is, just as we are.

Read it together, read it alone, read it well.

2021

THE WAITING OF
ASTER AMELLUS

Marisca Pichette

There's an art to studying the worlds that developed and faded to create ours. There is even a word. Of course, it is not a real word. Its creation depends upon the legitimacy of its meaning. The poet Chen Chen suggested its existence in 2020, when magic was not only needed but already there, flowing in LED waves from one eye to another.

To truly embody the art of knowingly un-knowing, re-knowing —there is a note of poeticism. A note of whimsy. Through these notes we begin to form a music of sorts.

Is there a way to accomplish this without poetry? I would argue that there is very little that can be satisfactorily accomplished without poetry.

The word is formed of two ideas: etymology and poetics. Combine these techniques and you have found what you seek: *poetymology*. Part past, part present. Part whimsy, part luck. Herein lies the artist's key to all other arts.

*

Asterisk is Swedish for star. Look at the Greek and find *asteriskos*: a small star. Above these lines hovers a small star. A star that really looks nothing like a star.

{Or maybe it does, a little. This star is the starting point—for *start* comes from the German for falling, and with one star we find that we are falling through space.}

An asterisk is truly a combination of words: *aster* (star, as we know) and risk. By placing them side-by-side, we are taking a leap. We are risking ourselves, flung headlong into space.

*

A fall through space reveals more about ourselves than the world around us. For there is no world. Space is emptiness.

{Empty comes from the Old English *mōt*. Moot. A meeting.}

The place that is empty is only waiting to fill.

*

We are here now, in space. Together, alone.
Around us, stars. Risks. Each a potential to fall, to be pulled into gravity and spin until all we can hear is silence and our thoughts.
Space exists to exact change. Space exists to confront
us with ourselves.
Alone. All one.
In space, everything is connected.

*

The Nectere were the original binders of the universe. They wound ropes from stardust and pulled the stars and planets into formation.

{Cosmos derives from *kosmos:* order, the world.}

The Nectere bound the cosmos together in a pattern that appealed to them. They tied gravity to itself using the sweat from behind their ears to grease the ropes. Ears have always been cosmically relevant.

{Ear derives from *auris*. *Auris*, aura, breath—which itself connects back to scent, and scent to sense.}

The Nectere ordered the cosmos using all their senses. With their eyes they tracked the placement of nebulae, with their noses exhaled the emptiness.

{For *ness* derives from *nasu*, nose.}

With their mouths they spoke to create the first echo.

{To speak is to draw from the Latin *spēs,* hope, and Old English *ēcan*, increase.}

In speaking into the dark, the Nectere increased the hope of all.

★

The Ekhe followed the Nectere once sound occupied the void.
Many believe one cannot see what isn't there, but the
Ekhe knew this was not the case.

{Void itself is connected of course to *voi*, see, so the Ekhe saw all
that wasn't there.}

Where the Nectere drew the universe into order, the Ekhe found
places for all things that the Nectere had forgotten.

{In this way they followed through with the Nectere's design—a
universe being a combination, designated of course by a central
controller.}

But the Ekhe—like the Nectere—were just one facet
of the many who braided stars into galaxies,
tying them off with clusters of moons.
The Ekhe turned to all that was dark.
They pulled blackness to life—black, a product of fire.

{The existence of stars required the presence of blackness. Without
it, the braids fell apart and planets lost their moons to the Edges.}

What was invisible carried its own significance to the Ekhe. They
were concerned with the weight of all that
the Nectere's eyes refused to see.

{Weight derives from movement. What is important is never still.}

The Ekhe gave us dark matter—for as *matter*, it is by definition significant—and dark energy, and black holes which carried their own profundity. When the Ekhe were finished the universe had shape and weight, light and darkness.

{But shape derives from *gesceap*, meaning little more than "external." And to be whole is to have a hole, and a hole is hollow, and a hollow is empty.}

And emptiness is always waiting for someone to arrive.

★

The Ripa placed themselves on the edge of the universe, erupting from crevices passed over by Ekhe and Nectere alike. Born from the limit, itself a place of violence, the Ripa continued breaking even as they grew. Their focus was on the fringes of places, on shorelines and cliffs.

{Shore comes from *shear*, from cutting and dividing.}

The Ripa's business was in finding places for all the things they did not like.

A place may be intended as a broad, open space—but the Ripa made only small, cramped places. They took their definition of place by removing the p to create lace, recalling *laqueus,* noose. And from lace they elaborated into *lacerate*, so all their cut-places were also mangled spaces—space mangled into place into lace.

{Yet if the l were removed, the result would be ace,
which comes from *as*—unity.
This would not be discovered until many years after
the Ripa found a place for themselves.}

The Ripa beat the ends of worlds until there were no craters left but those nestled deep in the pores of their own skin. These they turned to, at the shore of their age.

They beat themselves until all that was left was a ringing sound, filling the final resting place of their own making.

*

After the Ripa rang themselves into dissonance, the Restan came. Their objective was to travel the new cosmos. Their goal was to locate some place to rest at the end of it all. But as we know, travelling comes first.

{Rest is defined by distance: *ræstan*, league, mile.}

In travelling, the Restan encountered the binds that the Nectere had made. These they used to measure the distance they covered.

In measuring, the Restan brought peace to the cosmos—if for the moment. They measured planets and thus provided them with food (for a *mes,* from measure, is a portion). They measured galaxies and brought ceasefires—as the second half of measure is to be *sure*, free from all care.

The Waiting of Aster amellus

When the Restan came, they were welcome.
When they left, they were missed.
The Restan traversed the entire universe in this way,
until they came at last to the abyss.

{The abyss is not nothing. It is in fact *abussos*, bottomless.
In this way it is everything.}

{It holds more than either the Nectere or the Ekhe could ever
bind or see.
But as it is the bottom, it is *Boden*, earth.
And as it is less, it is *lēssa*.
Last.}

*

Aster amellus is the most common application of star
to something growing.

{Growth itself derives from green.}

Aster amellus is purple and green, where purple recalls in its
etymology the mollusks that once clothed emperors.

The *Aster amellus* is thus an emperor of a flower.

Its first name we know: *aster*, star.
Its second, *amellus*, means wonder.

Take a leap toward a star, and the result is self-evident.

Wonder. To find it, take a connected word: yonder.

Wonder is over there.
Wonder is at the intersection of *wont*—what we are accustomed to
—and *der*, a splitting, a peeling back.
Revealing what lies beneath the skin.

Alternate meaning: wonder translated back into Latin not as *amellus*
but as *miror.*
Mirror. Looking at.

Combine what is accustomed and the act of splitting and you get
mira—abundance
—and *irror*: marked with many dots.

Many stars.

A look in the mirror reveals the cosmos that lies beyond.
The stars that fill the emptiness,

waiting to be joined.

SUBDUCTION

Donika Kelly

We come of the earth, children of nickel
and iron. For a time, we were daughter/mother,
mantle/core: we roiled and burned, set fire,
were fire; we were wind and storm without water,
and nothing could separate us but us. For a time
we were an interior orbit, inevitable
as pressure and heat: Hadean.

    The mantle with a pip in the gap: let me go.
    In the core's mouth a tornado of flame.

I broke the surface as an ocean breaks, lanced
the blistered crust. Alone, I was a yawning,
a great rift. I cooled. Slow came the hardening—
accretion: the brittle crawl away from the hot ridge
of the past— a long time from home—then the abyssal
plain, the open floor. The core spun as if of gold, as if I'd
never left, a constant discontinuity, a flaring whir.

Of course.

    Whatever opens, closes. Whosoever leaves,
    returns, comes inexorable to subduction.

I've returned, mama, ready to be taken under,
swallowed into rock plastic with heat. I can't deny
the relief of being driven inward, the comfort
of a hand raised to no reply, subject again
to the familiar indifference of home.

AT HOME

R. Bratten Weiss

At night when no one is looking she
hooks her claw into the skin over her
ribs and slits the whole thing down the middle,
neat as a zipper. Then steps out.

All day she has been burning things down,
bat-wings unfurled in the smoky air. She
has swallowed the lances of men who
came to slay her. She is sick with them.

All her way home the blood drips from her gut,
ink black. Her blood splatters in hieroglyphs.
If the men with lances follow her they
will be unable to decipher them.

Now beneath the singed hide her flesh is pink
like a baby's. Like a new peeled peach.
Jeweled bangles glitter on her arm and she
remembers music on the water.

She remembers the touch of a hand when
she had hands, the touch of skin when she
had skin. She remembers red blood and skeins
of yarn wound about wrists, cat's cradles.

In the morning she will put her dragon
skin on again and crunch bones, but tonight
she dances. Her shadow on the wall doubles,
triples. She is one and many. And alone.

DRAGON

Alexander Walker

'Uret noticed that the dragon was broken, having only one wing; but his heart soared, for to him this was the perfect dragon, as all dragons are perfectly themselves.' – from a plaque in East Carlton Park

There. That volcanic pin tip
smouldering in the dark.
A focal point, aid to navigation.
Something to cling to.
Earlier this evening

I followed it all the way home.
Somewhere on the outer edge
of the atlas page, the words
here there be dragons
are scrawled out in the ash

it left behind.
It is summer, and the heat in your lair
is unbearable. All sulfur
and sweat and the scrape
of sharp scales. Too much.

Too close for comfort.

Laying back, eyes fixed
on something that neither of us can see,
you blow me a smoke ring –
trembling centre, fraying edges –

shoot through it a jet, gout,
spectral arrow. Disperse.
Dissolve. Destroy the only thing
you have ever given me. In this moment,
caught in the act of destruction,

you are so perfectly yourself.

ICARUS FALLS AND SITA FLIES

Peehu

Every night before I go to sleep,
I have this vision,
A little sight
of Sita lowering herself into the earth,
and Icarus flowing near the sun.

Both forced to be grown
The hubris of mortality set aside
Moving towards a death
they know nothing of
But death, they must embrace

I like to think
They happen in the same moments
On opposite ends
Of the same Earth

Sita lowers herself into mother Earth,
During night
As it is for her
A cold dread of longing
Her pride to be kept,

Peehu

She has no choice
So she falls to her knees
Begging to be reclaimed by the Earth

Icarus is carefully crafting his wings,
His hands full of blisters
From melting the wax
to be melted again
He knows the sun
For it is like the fire
Just larger and hotter
He knows what shall happen when he flies near it
His hubris doesn't let him back away
He flies near the sun and his wings melt
He falls to his death

While Sita fell directly into the Earth
And Icarus indirectly
Along the same day and same time
Sita and Icarus met there
Below the earth
In their mother's arms

Only to realise, they were but the same

THE MYSTERY OF US

S. Rupsha Mitra

Let us navigate through the blindness of our dusty
pasts perfumed in the fragrance of tinted mist,
let us hypothesise the body's beginnings, it's unexplored imaginings
– through the mystic crackle in the sky.
– and the fire of light
how the body is built
from membranes
born of water and fire, maybe in a certain reversal of ways when
the earth found the body and made its place within as if in the
garbagriha of its temple –
rotating
through seasons, and replenishing.
How the landforms emerged –
mounts as platoons fighting the strange decay of disease, barriers
and sheaths,
a vale, deep and rain-shadow
in between
– an oasis archaic
healing and revealing –
slushy yet skillful in preserving the ferocious uncensored longing,
blending with divinity.
A communion like an umbilical cord bound
with the universe in this self, in the human body.

WHITE NOVEMBER

Ojo Taiye

what may exist between time & grief, between memory & silence, is as beautiful as a rose bush cracking into brittle red earth. a sickle wind slashes grass in a room i thought was empty—i stretch the replay of a song across the year: where a girl who is dreaming becomes the girl in another girl's dream, momentarily forgetting that fireflies are indeed fairies. i wonder if in her dreams i can speak. i don't know who entered her without asking—my sister a swanned girl, long gone & in my hands, her memoirs cry & swell. nothing fills me like the sky dimming so fast it seems alive with the taste of a name worn thin. don't we all long to be less taciturn? or is it that everything living is also dying. a girl screams & a tree falls—i mean a stone falls through a line, landing somewhere within me. where does the crimson bird without girlhood return? the night is the night. for once, nothing is wrong—i listen to another man speak of desert & salt.

WHOSO LIST

Lucy Peters

We were taught to take care of desire
By tales that turned with a rustle of leaves
To pursue new shapes. By dark or by water,
Be aware that the lover you find
May be dappled strange: don't watch
From beneath your eyelashes, or if
You must, find her reflection in the river
Or the moon. There was a man
Left the pressed grass after his wife's shadow
And found a white snake
Rippling like her arched hip bone;
There was another went out to shoot
A scanty-legged, moist-eyed deer
And returned to his bed, where his child-bride
Lay startled dead in her tawny hair.
Someone's mute love fled to the wood
Where her loose lips filled with bees
Feasting on her tongue's nectar:
The crouching men had learned by now.
And we also learned not to follow the flash of a glance
Into indigo shade. We did not realise
That hunters might be lost in the nets

Of the trees. Forced to find rest,
We crawled into the quiet vines and moss
And the tree roots pressed us to the earth like thighs;
Blind mouths and velvet moths are very close
In the gloom, and trickling insects falter
Inwards like fingers; an ophidian sweep of hair
Reels over your throat and lizards
Scratch at your spine: and presently by surprise
The fur spidered across my ribs and the
Dangerous change jolted my own heavy legs
And by my new-narrowing eyes
I saw the speckled forest in purple and gold.

WATER TAKES THE PLACE OF ROPE

Jenny Mitchell

That's what I tell my children when they cannot sleep,
dreaming of their father, the day when he was trapped.
A group of men put water round his neck, pulled
until the water was so tight, he could not shout for mercy
so I screamed, 'Take the water from his neck'.
It tightened as they led him by the water through the town.
Men were told to pull the water till it strained, about to snap.
But water was so strong it began to chafe his skin.
Blood began to mix with water as I called his name. He turned,
despite the water pulling at his throat as if he was a hated dog.
His eyes grew dim with rope. He gagged and I was sure
he asked me for a cup of rope. It flowed, a stream nearby
made such a soothing sound as water round his neck was yanked.
Men pulled him to the ground beneath the oak.
No matter how I begged, the water was thrown up
to meet a sturdy branch. Men pulled the water
till his feet were lifted off the ground. I always end the story
with these words, 'Your father stands beside the rope and waves'.
I wonder if my children dream of water?

CADAVERS

Abduljalal Musa Aliyu

I was still wallowing in the abyss
Of adolescence when mother took
Me to a cemetery for a neighbour's burial

I asked her why they put the corpse
Beneath the earth against its wish
Like the night forces itself onto the day

The eloquence in mother's laughter almost
Ran into the ears of the attendees
She told me the first two men to ever pass

Through the gate between a woman's legs
Had a bloody fight & one killed the other
Took him to a dark forest; confused about

How to make the body fly on the wings
Of the winds. Two black birds appeared
From nowhere; the small one killed the big

& opened the earth with its pointed mouth
& lowered the body six feet beneath.

ਫੁੱਲ ਚੁੱਕਣੇ

Bal

We spent ninety years rehearsing our birth,
yet both unlearnt deep breath
shortly after leaving water.
Our structure changed,

when dirt held us up
I cut exposed orchid roots,
mistaking them for the deceased,
forgetting languages from when we were an alike species.

The decay resonated,
laid eggs in capillaries causing bumps.
Two burst vessels with no origin,
a mole marks the spot where a memory tunnelled into my knee.

I am an insect paralysed in dye,
an attempt to reflect your colour.
We try to make a moment still,

                              but wind sweeps matter

Bal

nausea induces a noteless song,
condenses on windows.
The garden wound oozes a sigh,
I wrap it in the jumper I wore where it left.

I ask Phulkari to mimic petals when they've never met you.
When squeezed, fabric burns to water,
another stream to ocean.
Stranded at land,

soil muffles my speech
explaining a faded scent.
They weave a suit created for scattering,
it reincarnates into rain

                              and nothing implodes.
                     As sand turns to sediment,
                 ash becomes washing up liquid.
          Do showers carry picked flowers from sea?

                    Do long-legged stems gain release
                     inside motes dancing in space?
                                    Facing sun,
                                music echoes.

                When dust is alive everything echoes,
               a mother-tongue indifferent to time.
                        Holding my own hands,
                    can't our years be heard?

THE ANGEL THAT CREATED IBLIS

afshan d'souza-lodhi

there are stairs that sit in the middle
of forests, going up to nowhere
coming down from everywhere.

we meet our angel sat at the top
waiting for her adopted son
to be graced by her presence.

she descends once every decade
sits on the steps, cries and then returns
to her place in the heavens.

in the beginning there was nothing
and then god said let there be light.
she shaped the light as one shapes
candy floss at children's fairs.
each layer of light creating shadows
from the previous layers until
darkness is created and intellect shines through –

      when you mother calls you 'a bright child'
      this is what she refers to.
but just as light cannot choose to bend,

nor can angels. they are devoid of nothing
but free will. they were created amongst
darkness to purify the world.

the story goes that this angel created these
steps to elysium the moment
her son was no longer a kept promise.

cycles ago she was commanded by her god
to clear the earth of jinn. the fire they bought
with them turned the earth into ashes
      and dust. that's where she first met
her son, blowing little darts of fire on
black marigolds by the sagar.
every time he hit one he turned
for approval from guardians
that were never there.
one day it was her, our angel, watching
the flowers attempt to dodge the fire and fail.
before the angels won, she spirited away
with him like he was hers.
masked the fire so all anyone would see
was light and gave him a name like
      the others. Iblis. she called him.
she taught him love, how to
be, do and live with it.
she taught him that
not all stairs have to have a destination,
but destinations need stairs to get to.

the angel that created Iblis

he fell in love with god as
poets fall in love with words that
don't belong to them – faithfully
unconditionally and not ever knowing
why. still. he was the light that only came
with shadows from fire. see fire is an event.
when you light a match and watch it burn
down to your fingertips there is
a moment you decide to blow it out.
there is a moment you don't.
that moment, when you don't
that's him. Iblis,
leaving impure thoughts
across those he falls upon.
he was supposed to be pure light,
existing only to shine bright and brighter
and do god's bidding.
     – he said no.

when god asked her angels
to bow down to her beautiful creation
of woman, Iblis said no.
how could he bow down
to anything other than his mother,
his mistress,
his god.
his love for Allah is what got him
expelled. his will was showing.
he, like the other angels

wasn't supposed to have one
and yet here he was refusing to bow
down to man and woman.
it didn't take god long to cast
the last remaining jinn back down
to spend eternity on earth
amongst those he hates.

Iblis now strides surrounding us.
his every step a manipulation
we have yet to come across.

the ash satan, the jinn, Iblis
is created from fire. it annihilates
through devastation and still amuses minds.

the next time you see something
spontaneously combust, know that
she, our angel, is waiting

at the top of steep stairs
with a bouquet of black marigolds,
for her son.

but Iblis never comes.

ROCKPOOL

Nicola Geddes

When did you live by the rocky shore?
years, or maybe decades ago
when did you walk on that rocky shore?
whenever the tide was low, was low

what was there on the limestone shelf?
old stories in fossils and holes through the stones
on what did you feed yourself, yourself?
spinach and samphire and mackerel bones

in the cliff-top pool, what did you find?
it had no name, no name I knew
a living thing I could see through
was it always there? was it there all the time?
there in a pool near Poll na bPéist.
its skeleton was lace, was lace

beneath the tissues of its skin
there pulsed the force of life within
I dipped a finger in its world
the creature and the ripples swirled

but it did not hide, it did not try
so far beyond its ken was I

did you see it since? did you find it again?
I found it in a piper's tune
on the lonely face of the setting moon
can you show me where? can you tell me when?
there in the sea green swell and the foam
as the tide turns round, and the waves come home

are we far away from the rocky shore?
we are near and far, and close enough
how do we find the rocky shore?
our bones are made of all its stuff

so now we watch the sky, the sky
we wait and see just what is showing
the air around us ripples by
beyond this fragile dome of knowing.

THE CHALK DANCE

Charlie Kite

Way Back

before
> lorry queues
> referendums
> *keep them out*

Kent was all chalk.

Sky, grass, river, all chalk
white bone dust, bone's rust, musty
air
wherever the wind blew.

Back Then

the Earth pushed. It did.
It heaved and sighed and moved and rolled in heavy breathing
and the land would grow

                                                        retreat

and grow again.

Each steaming breath from the hot blue core
sent particles crashing in the air.

It did.

bone dust, bone's rust
speck of white, night's breath
chalked life, rest's death

Passing time, dust danced together.
Passing time, people grew,
men, yes, women too, all dust and
chalk.

Ghosts in a ghost world.

Then
the
rains
came.

Rushing and roaring and raging and
drizzling and dancing and dashing and
spit, mist, downpour, deluge
drip, drip, dripping through them.

They were porous, then

the Men of Kent
the Kentish Men.

They marvelled at their rainbow sheen,
the oil slick colours in the puddles, pooling on their skin,
the glisten that would grow

                                             retreat

and grow again
in rain, after rain.

They needed colours.
They needed colours to play.

Green painted grass from drizzle
thick puddle grime for grizzled bark
hissing river swell from showers

They crashed chalk together.
Badgers first

                                            obviously

then mottled adders, russet foxes,
sanded dormice, flamed robins.

They hid their chalk bones so deep under

                        painted colours

                             perfected manners

                             home county gestures

that they could never be found.

But

                        on some nights
when the rain stops and a
bleached crescent moon peeks around the clouds
the Men of Kent
the Kentish Men
leave their houses in swelling crowds
and go into the Great Garden.

Charlie Kite

High Weald
North Downs
Vale

They undress their bodies with ditch water
marvel at their oily sheen
reveal the bone dust that lies beneath
and strip the world to chalk.

EXORDIUM:
DRAMATIS PERSONAE

Molly Beale

White Master is artist is lover is prophet is dealer is teacher is nurse and butcher. White Master is banker is plantation owner overseer overlord king of kings. White Master is ground sugar is loaf of bread is the bricks and the air we breathe. White Master is Mecca Bingo. White Master the City of London. White Master the monster under your bed the Chief Constable of Police. White Master laid the table before you were born and he will clean you up afterwards too. White Master is mist is flotsam and tide. Our Holy White Master is pestilence.

Mother Country in ancient infancy played. Her hillocks curved with grasses, big green trees that swayed with the currents above our heads. Colours, their lights disbanding from original objects, limits; suspending then dragging then blurring. Colours made more of themselves. Mother Country allowed body flow: flexing and stretching her streams into rivers, deltas. Now she is history, or what you want to be history. White Master voted himself in. Implemented intangible chains, pinned her in place with factories and grey things: prisons, legal courts, detention centres, military bases, shopping malls and museums. No longer searching for our spinning stars and suns, Mother Country looks into the nothingness made of herself: that inevitable core.

Fairies of Flame want to speak with your manager. These Fairies live, love and laugh. The fairies want to know what you're doing here? Like, where do you really come from? What are you doing on my property? Where's your permit? Just who do you think you are? Go back to where you came from. The fairies spent their gap year building schools for the cute kids in Africa! The Fairies are calling the cops. Fairies don't want any trouble. The fairies would really appreciate it if you didn't speak in such a harsh tone. You're just not understanding where the fairies are coming from. They didn't mean it like that. There's no need to think of yourself as any different: it doesn't matter if you're purple, green or blue! Fairies are colourless: monochrome magic. All working for the same sisterhood. The fairies can't help that they're crying. Fairies lean on their rifles and squint. Fairies pull the trigger.

ILIAD

Anne Chafer

Pain is the wire of history.
An oral history of loss, a family tree of violence.
A poet who sang to a poet who sang to a poet who sang
And so on until the poet who wrote.
In Catalan, sang means blood.
Blood from the heart of the poet who wrote
To the one who slept with the pain under his pillow
A dagger by his neck, Achilles by his tombstone.
And so on until a poet translated.
From song to voice to word.
And the pain spread, wires splitting,
Connecting the electricity of hopelessness
the catharsis of being human beyond the sea.
And so on until the poet who loved.
Cell to cell to cell we are the same, he said.
We are the bones of myth we are the same current,
the shatters and remains of a Trojan ditch
in the way we find it hard to breathe.
And so on until the poet who read.
I cried in the library that day.
The scribble on the margins said "Achilles – emotion."
I finally felt the static shock of recognition
and printed it on my skin to remember the dead.
And so on until the reader was you.

ELEVEN EXHIBITS IN A BETTER NATURAL HISTORY MUSEUM, LONDON

Jenny Blackford

First published in Strange Horizons *September 2020*

1. Shards of the engraved roc egg
sent to Elizabeth I by a devoted suitor
from the deserts of Arabia, displayed with
eyewitness accounts of the Virgin Queen
on the back of the great bird
over Loch Ness,
hunting the monster.

2. A perfect emerald the size and shape
of a whale, left high and dry
when the flooded Amazon receded
in the winter of 1797.

3. A rat king from Siberia, gift
of the Czar, twelve tails tangled,
twelve bodies thin as cardboard
snap-frozen in the blizzards
called down by Baba Yaga
when Napoleon marched on Moscow.

4. The preserved remains of a bronze giant
dredged from an undisclosed location
off the coast of Crete. A hand-lettered sign
taped to the explanatory text explains,
in red, why the Greek government
needs the metal marvel repatriated,
threatens Britain with the wrath of Zeus.

5. A life-sized three-headed dragon
based on fossilized bones
from hip, skulls, and tail
and a patch of wing membrane
still iridescent despite the Deluge.
All three heads breathe fire every hour.

6. A giant beanstalk extending
from the sub-sub-basement
up through the fifth-floor cupola.
No one has climbed it past the roof
since the Curator of Plants disappeared
a hundred years ago.

7. A baby unicorn
complete with candy-cane striped horn,
employing the most careful taxidermy
of the late 19th century.

8. A daguerreotype of the yeti matriarch
who led an Imperial French expedition
to safety across nine wide crevasses.
The notice claims that she died,
groaning in bliss, of a surfeit of cheese.

9. The frogshark of doom
whose squamous emanations
(even as she floats in her formaldehyde tank)
send random visitors into eldritch visions
of the Armageddon of the Elder Gods.
No Curators of Amphibians
have retained their sanity
for more than a year.

10. Five fragments
of the green-cheese meteorite
thought to have caused the death
of most of the dinosaurs.

11. Down in the stacks, unseen
by day-visitors, old Nessie's head
mounted on a gold-crowned shield,
beside live video of her descendants
frolicking in the royal loch.

YOU ARE

Lea Harper

among the seventy sounds
the crows make to interpret the world

a syllable between tree and storm
something rootless, unpredictable.

If the one who fed Elijah in the wilderness
fires rotten food at you
(acorns, wolf scat, road kill)
you ought to be grateful.

He's dark lord of this perch,
arrived millions of years before you.
The territory's his.

An Arapaho noble donned a raven feather
and survived the white man.

Even princes know
if The Tower ravens leave
the Kingdom falls.

The crow's curious eye
is the bead that threads the world,
his cackle, an old fire
branded in the pools of memory.

Corvus corax corone:
Companion of God, return.
The earth has dried up.

Life is short, a wing span
measured by your indecipherable shadow,
a shiver of wind, your black diamond kiss.

*It is believed that "if the Tower of London ravens are lost,
the crown will fall and Britain with it."

NAUPAKA PLANTS

Arun Jeetoo

Star-crossed lovers
across urban boroughs and mechanized landscapes
separated   &   imprisoned
by sea or mountain
        call on the gods
of forbidden love
Paka and Nau   ask them to birth
        The Naupaka plants:
        A flower that blooms in half.
Kahakai grows near the sea   Kauihiwa grows near the mountains
small and whitish   small and whitish
with purple streaks   her   with purple streaks   his
petals are half and low   petals are half and high
When placed together, it forms perfection
        the perfect love.
By the sea's mouth   by the mountain's back,
both lovers' rest the Naupaka on their palms
holding onto this sweet-bitter thing
a piece of each other
grows forever   grows forever.

It is believed that the Naupaka flower blossomed because of an ill-fated love affair between two students at a hula school in Kauai, where dating was forbidden.

49

HERB OF THE SUN

Jay Délise

Did you hear
You must have heard

Muh and them saw shooting stars

Last night
On the porch
You know
Where we eat sometimes
When outside is cooler
Than inside

Anne shot right up
Like a firecracker
Pointed to the sky
And the sky started dancing

Seem like
It was doing it just for us
Reds and blues
Jackie said she saw god in the clouds
And she was smiling
I saw her too

Come here
Sit down
Let me tell you
Did you hear

The sun woke up yesterday
And told everybody she quit
Said she was tired
Of people frowning up at her
When she had her best dress on
So the trees went on strike

And the moon came out too
Middle of the day
Just to see what all the fuss was about
Tried to convince her to stay
But the sun wasn't having it
I don't blame her

And I've got to tell you
You had to have heard this
All the marigolds went missing
In the middle of October

Beverly said
It was because we all kept picking them
So excited that they grew
That we forgot
To plant any seeds

Herb of the Sun

I think
Somebody finally loved them enough
To keep them in the house
And didn't need to plant any more
Of the same thing

NOCTURNE

Manahil Bandukwala

Mehar calls these nights "Sohni raat,"   *Let's go, let's go.*

like chaand raat or Eid raat
where moon smiles from shadow
night where he watches river for sighting

of me. We lie together
and pray at each others' altars. I make mine
from clay, he makes his
from buffalo skull.

*

Fish nibble off the clay layer that collects
during my day in front of the potter's wheel,   *Time to go.*
think of me as algae
and rock.

Moon, she keeps my secret, stays
in shadow for three nights in the month. I sneak away

from house
from husband.

Riverbank squelches underfoot,
a quicksand, lost in white water. Elevate
my body with pot as life vest and kick   *Come on*
against the current.   *can't stop now.*

Shallow rocks scrape my stomach.
Something curls around my foot.

★

At the wheel today, my mother-in-law
wiggled a stick around
and called it a river snake.

★

Something slimy creeps up my leg.

Toes sink again and there is nothing,
just algae and clouds of riverbank mud. Water

black and white and every colour
but blue.   *Keep floating.*
Heavy and dark and everything but gentle.   *Let's keep going.*

Krrtch, krrtch, krrtch.

Nocturne

★

My sister-in-law said
there are crocodiles in this river.   *What if –*
She dropped a pile of unbaked clay

and its wet form settled around my feet.   *What if it gets me.*
Krrtch, krrtch. My father kicked a pile
of broken pot shards. Krrtch. This is the sound

my husband makes
when I don't listen to him. Krrtch.

★

I'm in a tunnel of rising water

rocks rise up and I land, loosen grip on my clay pot.
Wade with sari water-heavy.   *We're almost there.*
Something wraps a scaly hand
around my ankle,

washes off at the other end of the shore.

★

It is Sohni raat. Mehar watches the river

but morning light breaks
he sees no
bobbing head. Just wet lumps
of clay stuck to rock

tangles could be hair or seaweed

he waits. At noon
blue water brings him

a clay pot
unbaked.

LILITH IN ISOLATION

Anna Kate Blair

> *A serpent who could not be charmed*
> *Made its nest in the roots of the* huluppu-*tree*
> *The* Anzu-*bird set his young in the branches of the tree*
> *And the dark maid Lilith built her home in the trunk*
> ...
> *Inanna wept!*
> *(Yet they would not leave her tree.)*
> ...
> *Gilgamesh loosened the roots of the* huluppu-*tree*
> *and the sons of the city, who accompanied him, cut off the branches.*
> – 'The Huluppu Tree,' c. 2150 BC, trans. Diane Wolkstein[1]

1

Inanna, is every relationship an overcorrection for the one before?

Inanna, I was once aloof. I was always travelling to the underworld, always coming back. I was acting like you, acting *civilised*. I remember boxes of La Croix stacked high at Whole Foods, buying cutlery at IKEA. I made frozen yoghurt, poached salmon in rooibos tea. Inanna, I am renewed in each iteration, made maid again. I was once

---

1   *Inanna: Queen of Heaven and Earth*, translated by Diane Wolkstein, edited by Samuel Noah Kramer, New York: Harper and Row, 1983. The quote is from pp. 6-9, from 'The Huluppu Tree.'

too passive, too gentle, but I have sharpened myself now. Inanna, you are from a city built on bread and I live alone in a galaxy mapped with blood and satellites. I am waiting to see what will undo us. I am eager to find out.

2

Inanna, I dreamt that somebody was digging at my roots. I was struggling to stand, and yet I loved this unseen figure. In sleep, I felt a love so desperate it could only be grief. Inanna, I will wear black at my wedding and my tears will burst like pomegranate seeds, magenta, in your mouth.

Inanna, I woke to learn you had destroyed my tree.

Inanna, I am at the core of the tree. It is empty without me. Inanna, I am the sap in that tree, sticky, sweet, dripping. I suppose that means that I am yours. Inanna, I use your name like an incantation and it echoes through that hollow core, through time.

Inanna, cut wood doesn't last forever, and one day your throne will rot.

3

Inanna, I am looking back at you, now, from a wild, uninhabited place. Inanna, this could be exposure therapy for my separation anxiety. Inanna, I last touched another person when Mercury was in retrograde. I see you, on the internet, wearing earrings that hang like wind chimes, your plants balanced neatly atop the heater that clanged noisily in the early morning. I trace your moving mouth with my cursor and order flowers to be left at your doorstep. Inanna, I remember reading in your bed, in the trunk of my tree, drawing hearts with my fingers on your skin. I am attracted to anything disastrous. Inanna, I am trying to find your rhythm. I am haunted pixels, now, to you. I am in my body yet beyond it, on your screen, on mine, repeating. Inanna, you make me multiply.

4

Inanna, you are still my lettuce growing by the water. Inanna, I eat wild berries and words, but I have made bread for you. Inanna, you tell me that you want to taste the bread that I've made, that to measure the weight of it in your hands might carry an erotic charge. I lost myself in the hollow of your tree and I'm myself again, now, in these wild places, though I'm still baking you bread. Inanna, I imagine food in your mouth as I place it in my own. I will gather honey for you. I am unafraid of wild bees.

Inanna, the loaf that I made for you is round like the moon. It will stay full until you slice it.

5

Inanna, there is no wilderness like unrequited love, no courage to match continued feeling. I cry into my laksa, but there's no gravity here; tears and soup spill into air. *I hate her*, texts the *Anzu*-bird. There's no solidarity like platonic intimacy, but I'm a romantic. I could never hate somebody who has caused me so much pain.

Inanna, I love you, now, without idealisation. Inanna, I love you with anger. I love your flaws, your ruthless profiteering. Inanna, I have become a bad activist, forgiving your pipelines and highways, everything that you choose above a tree, above me. I skipped the union meeting on Zoom for fear of splintering at your face. Inanna, you are a true disaster capitalist, dressed as an activist, crowned as a goddess, writing a book with pandemic as hook. Inanna, you are like Slavoj Žižek but stealthier, more charismatic. Oh, Inanna, none of us are ideologically pure, and I'd still choose you as our leader. I love the chaos and the mess, the cruelty that you invoke yet turn away from.

Inanna, I heard, once: *we feel terror when we fall for one another.* I wish I could obliterate our differences, inhabit you as I inhabited our tree. Inanna, there are strange flowers that grow beyond your borders, your ordering gaze, your academic language, your self-congratulatory trip to the underworld, made possible by your servant and your ruthlessness.

Inanna, my dirtiest longing is my desire to take care of somebody else.

Inanna, I want to terrify you.

6

nice, like the razorblade
version of *kind*; *nice*, like
refusing to be angry so
you're never at fault; *nice*
like an *X* at the end of
a text message blowing
somebody off; *nice*
like diplomacy instead
of honesty; *nice*, a shrug
of *healthy boundaries*;
nice, like asking Gilgamesh

to cut down the tree; *nice*, like
photoshopping your hands
to appear clean.

7

Inanna, do you know that plants have been tried for occult collab-
oration? Inanna, I am the first witch. I am the enemy of pregnant
women. I have golden hair and my breasts are full of poison. Inanna,
I heard, once: *for a tree to go to heaven, it must send its roots to hell.* I
know you only wanted a bed and a throne, that I was one of many
nuisances, but, Inanna, I want to take it personally. You sleep, each
night, on my devastation. Inanna, sap still sings on the surface of my
forearms, and the ringed wood will not forget.

OVERTURE CON SORDINA

Jonathan Kinsman

for s.,
> *no apology is enough.*

i.

in the beginning was the word
  and the word was

                              NO

ii.

                    and from it life sang like iron
                              through the guts

    the cut and thrust

                              retched
                    forth in the wet slap
                    of bile against water

iii.

    all the earth perched upon your cervix
        how you trembled under its weight

                        we of infinite recursion
            nesting dolls
                ground at your insides

iv.

waiting for the break

star gasp
the blade that split
the shell
dripping yolk

you cannot make
anything without

v.

grit
you polished your ache
and it shines
blinding

vi.

a body a promise
and the nations cried
if you cannot keep it to yourself
we will keep it for you

crowned the babe with paper
blank verse

severed

Overture Con Sordina

vii.

and the child wailed winter

alone
on the mountaintop

my stone mother
a scream a scarecrow

howled the hangman
and his wife

bent double beneath the empty

viii.

madonna
we call her now

a precious thing

and you
my grandmother of the road ahead
our lady of ringing bells
queen under the earth

ix.

i lower my voice to you
whisper in the bloody dirt

hymn umbilical

Jonathan Kinsman

x.

                        name me clock
     and i will wind back his hands

  stop time
      unspeak

EVE REMEMBERING

Kait Quinn

after *Toni Morrison*

Eve remembers hunger, remembers pushing flesh
from her flesh, remembers candy-floss pink
cheeks rouged from her blood, remembers apple red,
remembers no woman came from a rib,
no bone could ever live without a womb to grow
and feed and shape it. Eve remembers the crisp
flesh between her teeth, the juice dripping sweet,
remembers revolution, remembers sacrifice,
remembers snake is synonymous with cheat
is entangled with lie. Eve remembers being chased
out of Eden into wilderness, remembers you
were there, remembers daisies and stars and explosions
pulsating between her thighs, remembers layers of rust
peeling off her limbs, skin wildflowered and gilded,
remembers spreading her wings, remembers screaming
and howling, remembers warm yellows and dusky blues,
the honey rich taste of freedom unfolding from her loins.
Eve remembers death singing softly, four little words:
ye shall be god(ess), as she drags out moon to dwarf the sun.

THE LESSON

C.B. Blanchard

Once there was Nothing and Nothing longed to touch itself.

Nothing fucked Nothingness and in the moment of pleasure
made Existence.
Bore a child. Brought it forth in pain. Gave of itself
for life to be.

In the afterbirth Nothing died.
Left Existence to grow up parentless and lost. Small
and screaming in the wreckage of the coming forth.
The very stars are blood stains still on the birthing bed.

Alone, Existence made their own creations
from Nothing. Formed
Bloody shapes in shaking hands. Splinters
of bone to hold them up.
Spat into their open mouths – oh
watched them begin, desperate for life
from that first screaming breath.

Existence learned from their parent
that to create requires a death
and sacrificed their children, not themself.

We are made of a corpse, and so,
we rot.

Bloody hearts in our chests and hunger in our mouths,
we repeat the lesson.

JANUS

Maroula Blades

You brush the softness with a sun song, move the doll quiet to a rich momentum. Notes peel back the cusp of imagination where Sapphics tease the mind in moon-shades, mauve light. A door opens to another reality; black embodies sweetness. In this place the truest moments can span a lifetime. You undress, shedding a Tyrian purple robe from your body. Honeydew crescents form in your beard; an assembly of liquid moments, a tamarind spa erupts to shine ebony skin. Naked you arch the back to drink from my warmth. Your tongue, a key that unlocks the aura in my body's core; it escapes through your eyes, as you turn your head to Janus Geminus. His face is pale, ribbon-smooth. He waters with crystal kisses. In the dark, his chin matures, but the hair is fine like spring grass. I look to the moon; it casts threads of light. A masculine silhouette kneels on the cream tulle drapes that hang from the canopy of our four-poster bed. You radiate a powerful life-force. Five caryatides come to life in the room and walk towards us in sultry light, hips swishing in pastel silks. They press their faces into the gauze, gently blowing their strawberry breath through the perforations, as you whisper to them, "Would you like some?" I stretch under the touch of petite hands. Red satin folds, I squeeze all that is within me, reaching the point of no return. Sublingual moans. The cloth moves in waves. Fingers stroke the movement of lips, orchids open; petals fall to skin. Every cell lifts on our nakedness. Within the rush buds accelerate in growth to full bloom. A mass of autumn-coloured hair falls to caress and coat me with kisses. Beautiful. My face is covered with She Nectar. Pheromones scent the air. An aperture widens, a new beginning settles. The lover in you wades within me, as you gently rock deeper and deeper. You reach the source; it splashes forth. I am held from within by your love. I rise for you to sip from the new hot spring. The Venus bone is soaked in nectar. You murmur your desires. The greed in your thirst renews the spirit. You harvest the love; red poppies open, dropping seeds. The sirens tiptoe backwards into the night to resume their previous muted positions. They sing a song of sighs that peters away into the still. You pull a silk thread from the drapes and string seeds together; within moments I have a black pearl waistband fastened around my hourglass form. I press my back into the mattress to feel the gems below the skin, as you slip from the bed, huge. You walk to the teak door; the rolling wind enters the room. Your long hair combs the air, fanning open, as if to wave good-bye. The door closes behind a bearded face. A tear rinses the night away to a close.

*In ancient Roman religion and mythology, Janus is the god of beginnings and transitions, therefore also of gates, doors, doorways, endings and time. He is usually a two-faced god since he looks to the future and the past, sometimes he is also depicted with four heads. The Romans dedicated the month of January to Janus.

CIXOUS RECOMMENDS/

Oakley Flanagan

Censor the body and you censor breath and speech at the same time.
Write your body. Your body must be heard.

Hélène Cixous, The Laugh of the Medusa.

a strong narrative of self-identity in which I eventually leave
the house looking visibly non-conforming / and I would never
get beaten up / laughing in the face / of anyone who'd shoot
me a second glance / hear / my pronouns / they / are believed
to be as natural as hers / no one contests / their / author / ship
of my gender / unfixed and yet essential / there / is no stormy
see / ha ha cargo / my body flowing with power and ridicule
decollated / neither / Perseus / his / shield / exist / no men can
on my island / they / have all been configured / into symbols
of my hermetically sealed existence / nobody / to muse about
me in the theoretical / sense doubting my validity in the real
stones thrown / become warmer bodies / held / I do not fear
the look-away horror / people love me and they / have no way
back / in this one I am / joyful and disruptive / no / they're / 'd
be nothing / left to disrupt the story / remains a fiction that is
to say an act / of will / falling / aberrant and creaturely
to stony ground / the outside hiss / his

WITCH BRAT

Jane Flett

Yesterday I was the witchbrat

I made a dark stew of blood and mercy
And fed it to the boy

He said What's for dinner?
I said Eat it. Hurry

It's time to avenge everything with teeth

Yesterday I broke the skin

The recipe worked this time
The hole opened & the boy fell

He said What's happening to me?
I said Hush. It's dinnertime

I baked cakes and pies and meat
Piled high on every surface

I spiked everything with the ooze

He gorged until giddiness came
Slick red drool on his chin

The witchbrat laughed and said
Swallow. It's time you belong to me

DEAD / ALIVE?

mandla rae

you hold my heart in your hands
gently
tenderly
you kiss it

softly.
you've never been one to squirm at the sight of blood,

it had to be me.
my clumsy hands would slip
and I'd drop it on the ground.
I'd vomit my breakfast
if I had to slice up your chest

but you are ever so delicate,
I thank you.

                             you catch my last breath in your mouth.

it was my time,
all of us have a time.

Do not watch my life with pity,

                when all you know is the story you created amongst
yourselves over thousands of years of mishearings and mistrans-
lations
your gods are merely gatekeepers,

              I do not speak your language.

had my love
also handed me her heart,
we both would have been food for the dogs.
rotting in the name of sentimentality,
that's no way for anyone to go out.

one day her time will come
and I can only hope she will have as pleasant a death as I.

if you give your heart away,
you die.
if you only take a heart,
you die.
if you give yours and receive someone else's,
the universe is kept in balance.
and still,
you die.

do not fear Death,
she is one with Living.

REMAKING OF A WORLD

Sophia Freire

Once upon a time there was City. In City there was a girl.

City was a wide, winding thing of twisted metal and broken glass. It was thick with many layers that descended down deep. City's metal broke the bones of Dreamers to build its body. Their blood would spill on cold concrete and make it warm. Such was how City fed.

The girl never slept. Her dreams undissected.

The length and depth of City she wandered. She crushed bulbs between her teeth, their jagged edges soft inside her. The endless stream of lights bubbled in her veins. Another heartbeat thumped in her mind.

Two hearts, too much blood. It burst the lining of her uterus. It seeped into concrete pores, coated sharp edges. It drowned the whole of the City.

Dreamers slept without pain.

No bruises. No cuts.

No change is welcomed.

The freed dreamers found the girl still kneeling, still bleeding. They grounded her down. Meat and bone crushed into earth and stone.

The red drowned gray, then green swallowed red. The Green remained. Cold turned warm. Sharp and jagged turned soft and growing.

Dreamless city to Forest. People slept, dreamed, and grew under soft canopies. We walk on her bones, We've forgotten the girl who bled us a new world.

CONTRIBUTOR BIOGRAPHIES

Marisca Pichette

The Waiting of Aster amellus

Marisca Pichette is a bisexual author living and teaching in Western Massachusetts. She writes speculative fiction, nonfiction, and poetry, and works to highlight marginalized voices. Her work has appeared in *Daily Science Fiction, PseudoPod*, and *Room*, among others.

Donika Kelly

Subduction

Donika Kelly is the author of *The Renunciations* and *Bestiary*. She is a Cave Canem graduate fellow and a founding member of the collective Poets at the End of the World. She is an Assistant Professor at the University of Iowa.

R. Bratten-Weiss

At Home

R. Bratten Weiss a freelance academic and organic grower residing in rural Ohio. Her creative work has appeared in numerous publications, including *Two Hawks Quarterly, Presence, Connecticut River Review, Shooter, New Ohio Review, Slipstream*, and *The Seventh Wave*. Her collaborative chapbook *Mud Woman,* with Joanna Penn Cooper, was published in fall 2018. Her chapbook *Talking to Snakes* was published by Ethel Zine and Press in summer 2020. She is the winner of the 2020 Helen Schaible Memorial Sonnet Contest, Modern category.

Alexander Walker

Dragon

Alexander Walker is a writer of poetry, fiction and nonfiction based in the UK.

Peehu

Icarus Falls and Sita Flies

Peehu is a young poet of 14, deeply interested in myths all around the world. They love drawing parallels between stories around the globe for it interests them to see how similar humans are. Based in India, their poetry is not encouraged by most people but their mother who is very appreciative of it.

S. Rupsha Mitra

The Mystery of Us

S. Rupsha Mitra is a student from India with a penchant for writing poetry. Her works have been published or are forthcoming in Fly on the Wall Press Magazine, Hebe Poetry, Muse India and North Dakota Quarterly.

Ojo Taiye

White November

Ojo Taiye is a young Nigerian who uses poetry as a handy tool to hide his frustration with society. He also makes use of collage & sampling techniques.

Lucy Peters

Whoso List

Lucy Peters' poetry and fiction have appeared in *Mslexia, Strix* and *The Citron Review.* Her writing won second place in the Vogue

Talent Contest, and has been shortlisted for the Bridport Prize for Flash Fiction and longlisted for the Bath Flash Fiction Award.

Jenny Mitchell
Water Takes the Place of Rope
Jenny Mitchell is winner of the Folklore Prize, the Aryamati Prize, the Segora Prize, a Bread and Roses Award, the Fosseway Prize and joint winner of the Geoff Stevens Memorial Prize 2019. A debut collection, *Her Lost Language* (Indigo Dreams Publishing) is one of 44 Poetry Books for 2019 (Poetry Wales), and a Jhalak Prize #bookwelove recommendation. Her second collection is called *Map of a Plantation* (IDP).

Abduljalal Musa Aliya
Cadavers
Abduljalal Musa Aliyu is a poet, school teacher and short story writer. He lives and works in Zaria, Nigeria.

Bal
ਫ਼ੁੱਲ ਚੁੱਕਟੇ
Bal is a West Midlands-based Punjabi poet studying at Bangor University. From A.K. Ramanujan and B. Prabha, to Jenny Holzer and Hetain Patel, she appreciates a range of artists whilst keeping no one free from critique. With an evaluative eye, typography influences her work's playful philosophy; it seeks to balance the multitude of spaces she belongs to. You can find her website at bal.gallery

afshan d'souza-lodhi
the angel that created Iblis
afshan d'souza-lodhi was born in Dubai and bred in Manchester. She is a writer of scripts and poetry and was commissioned to write and

direct a short film for Channel 4 and a radio play for BBC Sounds. afshan is currently a Sky Writes writer-in-residence for Rotherham and is also currently developing a TV series with Sky Studios. Her debut poetry collection 're:*desire*' (Burning Eye Books) has been longlisted for the Jhalak Prize (2021).

Nicola Geddes
Rockpool

Originally from Scotland, Nicola Geddes is now based in the west of Ireland where she works as a cellist and tutor. Her poetry has been published and broadcast widely. She has won or been short-listed in several competitions and awards, including winner of New Irish Writing in 2019.

Charlie Kite
The Chalk Dance

Charlie is a cross-genre off-centre writer, focusing on nature in the modern world, magical realism, and individuals and communities in change. Since 2015 he's had his plays performed at the Camden Fringe, Edinburgh Fringe and VAULT Festival, and has previously been shortlisted for the Papatango Prize. As a poet and fiction writer, he recently won the Oxford Review of Books' Short FIction Competition. Currently he's studying Creative Writing at Oxford University.

Molly Beale
EXORDIUM: Dramatis Personae

Molly Beale (@Mollygbeale) is a poet from Peterborough. *An Abolitionist's Fairytale* is their ongoing project examining white femininity and supremacy in the UK using fantasy and fairies. They recently completed a masters in creative writing poetry at the University of East Anglia and are currently working as part of the University Publishing Project. Molly's had work published elsewhere by *Datableed*, *Whatever Keeps the Lights On*, *Quince Magazine* and *New River Press*.

Anne Chafer
Iliad
Anne Chafer is a Catalan translator, writer and postgraduate student with way too many interests. Some of them include Homeric epic, classical reception, Taylor Swift, 19th century US literature, singing, and playing The Sims. Juggling everything together does pose a bit of a problem. Her work has been published in *Núvol, Exeposé* and *Varsity*, and she is currently studying for a Masters in Classics at the University of Cambridge.

Jenny Blackford
Eleven exhibits in a better Natural History Museum, London
Jenny's poems have appeared in Australian and international journals and anthologies including *Westerly, Going Down Swinging, Strange Horizons* and multiple *Rhysling* anthologies. Her poetry prizes include first place in the Thunderbolt Prize for Crime Poetry and twice in the Humorous Verse section of the Henry Lawson awards. Her latest collection from Pitt Street Poetry is THE ALPACA CANTOS.

Lea Harper
You Are
Lea Harper is an award-winning singer-songwriter and the author of two collections of poems, All That Saves Us and Shadow Crossing (Black Moss Press). Her work has been widely published in

literary journals and anthologies in Canada, the U.S. and the UK. She lives on a lake in Canada, in the Haliburton Highlands, 3 hours north of Toronto, where she's completing her next book of poems and first novel.

Arun Jeetoo

Naupaka Plants

Arun Jeetoo is a English teacher from North London. His words appear in *The London Reader*, a gallery in Cardiff with *LUMIN Journal*, Civic Leicester's *Black Lives Matter Journal* and *The Best New British and Irish Poets 2019-2021*. He was a participant in Waterloo Press' LIT UP: Poets of Colour mentoring scheme where his debut pamphlet *I Want to Be the One You Think About at Night* was published by Waterloo Press (2020).

Jay Délise

Herb of the Sun

Jay Délise is a poet and performer creating in the combined world of theatre, poetry and storytelling. A native of the Jersey Shore, Jay has performed at The United Nations, The Schomburg Center, The Pulitzer Center, and Carnegie Hall. Her work has been highlighted around the world and in publications including *Afropunk, Broadway World, Vagabond City, Glass Poetry Press* and *Huffington Post*. Her book *tenderhead*, debuted at number 1 in poetry audiobooks.

Manahil Bandukwala

Nocturne

Manahil Bandukwala (she/her) is a Pakistani writer and artist. Her most recent project, Reth aur Reghistan, is an exploration of Pakistani folklore interpreted through poetry and sculpture. See her recent work in the *Malahat Review, CV2, Briarpatch, Augur,* and other places. She is a member of VII, an Ottawa-based collaborative writing collective.

Anna Kate Blair
Lilith in Isolation

Anna Kate Blair is a writer and arts worker from Aotearoa. She has recently had work published in *Archer, The Lifted Brow, Meanjin, Lucy Writers' Project* and *Reckoning.* She holds a PhD in History of Art and Architecture from the University of Cambridge.

Jonathan Kinsman
Overture Con Sordina

Jonathan Kinsman (he/him) is a trans poet from Manchester. As well as being founding editor of Riggwelter Press he is also a BBC Edinburgh Fringe Slam finalist. His debut pamphlet, *&,* was joint-winner of the Indigo Dreams Pamphlet Prize 2017 and his second, *witness,* was published by Burning Eye in 2020.

Kait Quinn
Eve Remembering

Kait Quinn is a law admin by day and a prolific poet by night. She studied creative writing at St. Edward's University in Austin, TX and her poetry has appeared in Polemical Zine, Chestnut Review, VERSES, New Literati, and various anthologies. She is also the author of the poetry collections A Time for Winter (2019) and I Saw Myself Alive in a Coffin (2021). Kait currently lives in Minneapolis with her partner and their regal cat Spart.

C.B. Blanchard

The Lesson

C.B. Blanchard is a queer Nonbinary writer from another world. They love taking fairytales and making them gayer and weirder. You can keep up with them on twitter @BridhC and https://www. facebook.com/CBBlanchardauthor/.

Maroula Blades

Janus

Maroula Blades is an Afro-British writer/poet living in Berlin. She was the first runner-up in the 2018 Tony Quagliano International Poetry Award, and the winner of Erbacce Poetry Prize 2012. Works were published in *The Caribbean Writer*, *The Good Journal*, *Words with Jam*, *Abridged*, *The London Reader*, *Ake Review*, *Harpy Hybrid Review* and by Peepal Tree Press among others. In September 2020, Chapeltown Books released her flash fiction collection *The World in an Eye*.

Oakley Flanagan

Cixous Recommends/

Oakley Flanagan is a writer and poet. As a playwright: 'This Queer House' (OPIA Collective), *VAULT Festival*. A previous winner of the Out-Spoken Prize for Page Poetry, Oakley's work appears in *Bath Magg, Poetry London, Under the Radar* and *Wasafiri*, as well as anthologised work for *Hachette* and *Orion*. They are a winner of TLC's LGBTQ+ Free Reads scheme 2020 for their novel in progress 'Quercus'.

Jane Flett

Witch Brat

Jane Flett is an over-excitable pervert and odd witch. Her writing has been commissioned for BBC Radio 4, anthologised in the Best British Poetry, and Highly Commended in this year's Bridport. She's the founder of Queer Stories Berlin and one half of the riot-grrrl band Razor Cunts.

mandla rae

Dead/Alive?

mandla rae is a Black, Zimbabwean, Agender & Queer writer and creative type. Floating through the intersections of race, gender, sexuality, (lack of) mental health, class & foreign-ness, mandla is a leaf of love. Obsessed with archives and storytelling, they like to play with words and often make work that draws from their personal experiences/heritage, to prove that they exist and create conversations and connections with their audiences.

Sophia Freire

Remaking of a World

Sophia Freire was born in Brooklyn, New York, and currently resides in New Jersey. She is a graduate of Ramapo College of New Jersey. She enjoys reading and writing poetry and speculative fiction. She is mother to one human child and two cats.

This book and future 3 of Cups Press projects were made possible because of a generous donation from Chris Roberts.